Notes from the Underground

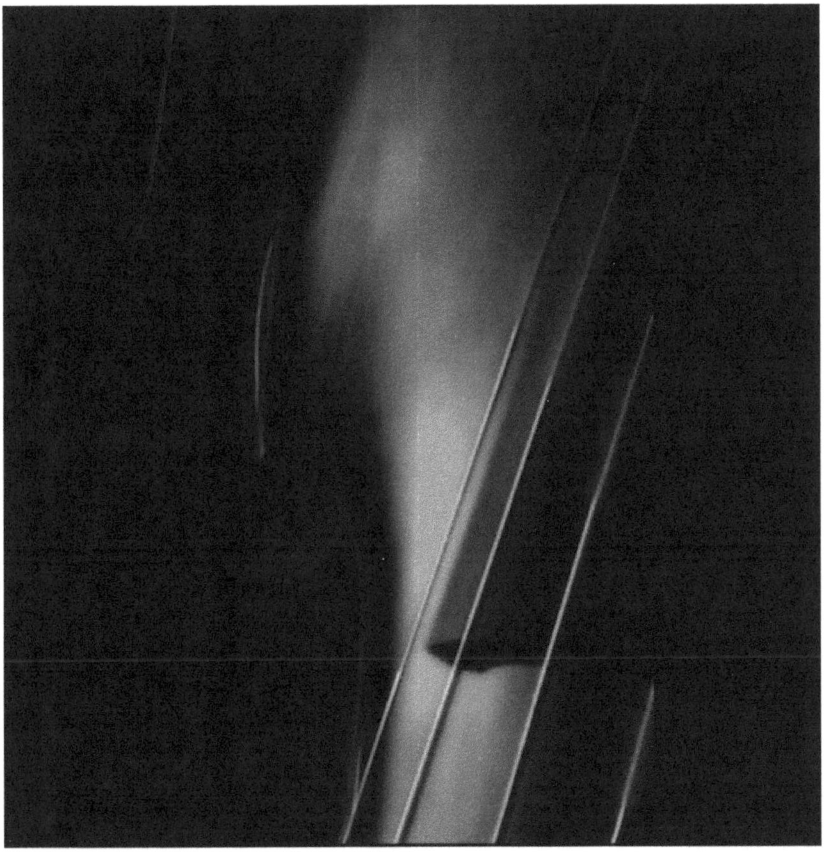

Preston Touchstone

Notes from the Underground

Copyright © 2024 by Coosa Books

ISBN: 978-1-7320782-4-6

All rights reserved. No part of this book may be reproduced or transmitted in any form or by any means without written permission from the author.

Dedication

This collection of poetry is dedicated to the memory of those brilliant poets of the Harlem Renaissance and the Black Arts Movement, who lit the fuse and continue to inspire my love of poetry.

Table of Contents

Jazz..1

It's A Jungle Out There 3

Jazz For Breakfast..................................4

State of the Tenor..................................6

2 A.M...9

Swing Time..11

To Kill A Brick....................................13

Trilogy..15

Like Sonny..17

New and Old Gospel.............................19

Mr. Gone..21

The Sound I Saw.................................23

Mr. Rivers...25

Miles Mode.......................................27

The Audition......................................29

Riffology...32

Monked...34

Homage...36

Trane ing In......................................38

Bud Powell..41

Legendary...44

Lazy Afternoon...46

Dig..48

Litter Box Blues..50

Revival..52

Andrew Hill Interlude................................54

Left Hand Lacey...55

Hooked...57

Miles to Go...59

Elegy for a Pharoah...................................61

I Remember..63

Jazz Sketch...64

Me n' Mingus..66

Abstrakt..68

Jesse B. Semple (Alternate Take)..............70

After Hours..72

Jazz

Now, that was music
they chime
in unison
like minds commiserating
with fellow
weathered constituents
arguing the facts
discourse with passion
positing knowledge
of the original music
It don't mean a thing
if it ain't got that swing
their precious rare sides
tucked tightly under arm
Ears open
Cheshire grins
remembering trips
on A train
uptown
recounting tales
of cutting contests
and famous jam sessions
A veritable who's who
of those that blew
Satchmo

or Miles?
Prez or Bean?
Sheets of sound
or a Saxophone Colossus?
Straight ahead Jazz
with a sensible swing
or chaotic freedom
of the new thing?
In the immortal words of
Ornette Coleman and
for the folks who
still don't know
This is our music

It's A Jungle Out There

Real talk
clears his throat
eyes tight
brim dropped
An Alpaca packing heat
Camel walkin'
copacetic ambulation
soft spoken
smooth talkin'
to Lou Donaldson's
Blueswalk
and other
soulful
Boo ga loo joints
trading in
unfiltered squares
for cigar smoke
Tommy gun
and a brand new suit
This cool drink of water
just landed a gig
workin' the door
at the most exclusive
Jazz club in town
After midnight
the jungle comes alive

Jazz for Breakfast

My morning constitutional

fried bologna

burnt on the edges

three scrambled eggs

a bowl of hot black coffee

my breakfast chaser

til rare side commences

Needle drop

and here it comes

The pop

the crackle

spillin' into anxious auricles

Wow(ed)

and flutter(ed)

pass the butta

Oh, how I love

the sound of vinyl

Chick Corea at the piano

Straight Up and Down

Boss Horn

Blue Mitchell on trumpet

Aloysius Foster

at the drums

Gene Taylor on bass

Junior Cook on Tenor

Julian Priester
on bone
Ahhh...

Listen to those unison lines
gotta crack a window
let the swing get out
but, I'm rushing
just a little bit
Hold up...
Let's back it up
Blue Note classics
breakfast on the table
Me, blowin' modes on
a bowl of hot black coffee
improvising over
Chick's solo
a lil impromptu vocalese
in between sips
black, no sugar
waiting for that caffeine kick
so, I can get bizzy
tighten up my ambitious
head on out
handle my bizness
But, before I do that
just one mo hit of Chick
and this delicious coffee

State of the Tenor

Jazz connoisseurs
jumpin' outta windows
throwin' melodious fits
on harmonic binges
teetering on edge
of improvised reason
This…
Tenor madness
infectious
addictive
brash boss tones
seeping deep
into bones
the coolest among them
The hip
the informed
who swung before
on yearly pilgrimage
paying homage to musicians
who took the music forward
Tales of the Tenor
Let's get ready to swing!
Horn men
to your corners

gettin' down
to brass (at)tacks
Of epic bandstand battles
and famous
jam sessions
of cutting contests
and trading eights
Big time
showdowns
twelve bar breakdowns
sweat drippin' from
nervous brows
These cat's cookin'
swingin' low
blowin' every note
they knew
and a few that sneaked in
If you can't cut it
they'll show you
the door
Prez n Bean
Big Ben Webster
Long Tall's
and Little Giants
chasin' measures
and time signatures
hard bop themes
blues

undercover
from West coast cool
to East coast modal
Sir Sonny Rollins
blowin' midnight stars
across imaginary bridges

A Wise One
called Coltrane
heralding
A Love Supreme
Inquisitive cats
bowing to
a modern day Pharaoh
counting off
the sound
to come
Archie Shepp
and Sam Rivers
riffin' their brand
of ugly beautiful
legendary cats
titans of the Tenor

2 A.M.

Only the lonely
congregate here
night breeds
and early risers
ascending
descending
quiet mourning
the sounds of Jazz
coloring steps
every stride
smooth
and in time
even their shadows
swing cool swagga
their laid back
a late night
lazy
loose
chasing the evening's
solitude
In dark of
small hours
silky silhouettes slide
with effortless grace
to hard bop strains
like shades pulled taut
outstretched limbs

of unencumbered ebony

these last of the twilight
jazz syncopators
glidin' against worn
mahogany floors
with their uneven heels
and educated soles
An intermingling
of black n' blues
A final cut of the rug
one last farewell
lights go dim
A soul serenade for
blue people only

Swing Time

Droppin' the bottom
chasin' the cool
settin' the groove
The rapid pitter patter
of syncopated brushstrokes
splattering rhythms
with ambidextrous precision
swishing over well worn
weathered skin heads
and cymbals
Painting percussive bars
in double time
Copacetic chatter
swingin'
til it's swung
diggin'
til it's dug
ridin' the cadence
An intermingling
of Jazz
a splash of scatology
vocalized blowin'
caterwauling coolness
with breakneck ease
Steady
In a hurry
Ella bringin'

the vocalesed swing

Straight
raw Dawg
without the chaser
don't look now
but tha cat's
out the bag
A St. Louis Blues
hip
uptempo
Ensemble and Voice
What a sublime combination

To Kill A Brick

It takes lots of pressure
constant
continuous
ferocious
and furious
straight out the gate
tones tumblin' tumultuously
from horns trading fours
like jackhammer bursts
swingin' brilliant
buoyant colors
no afterthoughts
or notes left over
just precisioned perfection
fast forwarded in real time
4/4 locomotion
full steam ahead
the cat's out the bag
My man must've been gifted
by Gabriel
Woody blowin' the house off
its foundation
cool
concise
cogent lines
whether in unison
or fading flawlessly

into solos

blowin' bars out the door

seamless

impeccable

questioning

then answering

conclusion reached

Trilogy

Up jumped Spring
from Chick's piano
Lotus Blossoms swingin'
A Kenny Dorham
Underwater strut
Chick
gettin' slick
turn up the volume
commiserating
with hip young prodigals
second go round
ensemble gettin' down
elastic
bombastic
McBride and Blade
settin' blistering paces
double stops and
paradiddles droppin
Monk & Miles
hard bop originals
triumvirate drivin'
each side angled
equilateral
chasin' Corea manifestations
of improvisation
a game of changes
chordal

modal
a cool copacetic
hide n seek
here comes the catch

Jazz head connoisseurs
groovers and shakers
Shades of Dejohnette
and Holland
open
adventurous equilibrium
bouncin' buoyantly
Eiderdown
or up
All Blues & Ballads
on display
Pastime Paradise
on parade
Alive
and killin' it
the swing comin'
straight out the oven
500 degrees
piping hot
golden brown
edges simmerin'
So watch your fingers

Like Sonny

Saxophone Colossus
hangs
over his bed
horn case opened
Tenor poised
upon altar exalted
deep in consecration
Bald head
Soul patch
Sir Rollins like
paying homage
to his idol
searching for comfort
under isolation of bridges
crossing Chelsea
just to get conscious
daily practice
twilight sessions
where he blows
and takes bows
before silent applause
honing his craft
Half steppin' upwards
ascending octaves
reaching for the stars
approaching

Tenor Madness
blowin' inspired notes
out of the blue
bold colors
textured tones
angled sideways
shiftin'
and surgin'
blazin' intoned
solitary phrases
played in obscurity
like Sonny
use to play them
One day he'll get there

New and Old Gospel

Jackie's alto
and Ornette's trumpet
quoting chapter and verse
straight between the eyes
No pullin' punches
no sugar coating
shoutin' soliloquies
edifying the divine
How shall they hear
without a preacher?
Take me to the river
let's wade a little
bathing in Bethesda
the waters are troubled
Outside
the status quo
improvising sermons
on the edge
on the spot
outrageous

John the Baptist
like tactics
bringin the fire and brimstone
rebellious exhortations
transforming
negro spirituals

into Blue note originals
Hard bop swing
fueling fiery hymnals
testifying
blowin that avant garde
ugly beautiful
breakin' it down
line by line
precept by precept
Swing you sinners
here comes the benediction
set concluded
closing time
Altar call

Mr. Gone

Wayne's thang
tha hard bop swing
droppin' halves
and quarters
improvised chatter
tuned up
and makin' change
whether upstage with Miles
matching unison lines
note for note
or minding his own
Mr. Shorter
out of order
blowin' somewhere
between Rollins
and Trane
over modal colored rainbows
cogently informed
blues drenched originals
leaping octaves
expanding registers
Betta hold ya breaths
we goin' under
diving bell first
into pentatonic depths

with tenor and
soprano saxophone riffs
inciting riots
painting smiles on faces
fastidious gazes
cats in corners
collapsing into conniption fits
slappin' fives
feet tappin' syncopated rhythms
footprint's imbedded
Took his Master's
at the University of Blakey
his PH.D under Dr. Miles Davis
An exegesis on
how to swing
Now c'mon y'all
show me your
Freedom Dance
Every time he plays
I see Africa again

The Sound I Saw

Sublime
transcendent
dulcet intonations
secular grooves
exquisitely ascending
something celestial
bordering on the spiritual
Notes winding indiscriminately
chromatic colors
climbing
acclivous
bottom(ed) up
crescendo
rungs rhythm a ning upwards
ever
unending
unadulterated swing
riffin' uptempo
In 4/4 time
the bounce
that drive
I can't put fingers on it
opening ears
so, I can hear a little clearer
ghost notes lingering
spacious
subliminal

re-birthing the cool
like when Miles
tugged on ear lobe
after a blazing solo

or Monk's impromptu soft shoe
when quartet is really swingin'
those abstract intangible moments
only perceptible when the senses
are honed and hittin'
No need to turn up
the volume
Just close your eyes
and listen…

Mr. Rivers

On the outside
of in"
the upswing
of the downbeat
this Avant-garde hip cat
a prodigious anomaly
goin' in nonstop
blowin' incongruous notes
and zig zag riffs
never played
the same note twice
asymmetric squeaks and honks
in and out of tempo
changin' it up
always keep'em guessing
resetting the clock
Keep up or get out
Forever tick tocking
time is money
subversively swingin'
over rhythms of elders
escaping into
alternate dimensions
extensions of self
B flat resolutions
if you're wondering why
C sharp for questions

separating the variables
then, solving for X
where right is wrong
and left is right

euphorically subliminal
a lyrical enigma
Solid gone
improvising spaces
on spontaneous quest
free jazz explorations
The game hasn't changed
just trying
sumthin' different
Cause if they figure you out
you're done for

Miles Mode

Farrell flexing on Soprano
in lieu of Tenor
searching
inner urges
surging
burning
full sprint uptempo
following in
footsteps of a giant
Miles Mode
a Coltrane original
canoodling Milesian
modal coolness
unearthing elders
the birth of cool exhumed
arrayed in new clothes
a free bop groove
swing intact
taut
intense

This quartet cookin'
tearing through measures
bogarting bars
fiery solos
notes incendiary
dig the way his horn

just hums
turning on
the afterburners
a locomotion of keys
and fingers
lips pursed
embouchure perfect
Bass man bottom ing
the tonic
walkin the dog
on leisurely stroll
Louis Hayes
double time swingin'
teasing
the rhythm
Pianist comping
waiting his turn to solo
One more go round
then, restating the theme
last chorus
It's time to go home

The Audition

It's not the size of the horn
it's how you swing it
said disgusted
sax man
to group of women
gigglin' across the room
unzipping leather case
shoving alto in
cramming extra reeds
into empty pockets
Sure looks pretty
small to me
one of them chuckles
under breath
alcohol
coloring her speech
laughter soaking
synthetic grin
These self proclaimed
Birdies from Bayside
on casual weekend
gallivant
to Dewey's Saturday Nite
Jazz showcase
where would be Coltrane's
and Charlie Parker wannabe's
ply their lyrical wares

in hopes of
securing
a gig
with the house band
steady dollars
attention from the ladies
and all the booze
your gut can carry

Smooth Jazz don't fly here
try Salt Peanuts
or Caravan
His piece...
A rousing rendition
of Feelings
in swing time
an uptempo cooker
with plenty of heat
but obviously not
their cup of tea
or so it seemed from
the lukewarm applause
and awkward stares
Maybe next time
come back in a week
Manager's cigar giving
him a headache

along with extra chatter
from the next cat
sittin' in
and the sting of women's
laughter singin' after him
as he exits Dewey's
showcase door
His horn tucked firmly
under arm
pride left lying on the
showcase floor.

Riffology

Streams of bop dreams
drippin' promiscuously
from virginal horn
Another young lion
on first take
gettin' cherries popped
modal membranes
pushed in
tautness torn
tension released
Peep that trail
of hip rufescent fluidity
flowin' from
embouchureal technique
In thru tha nose
out thru tha mouth
lethal lippin'
chords and crimson oozin'
notes of sanguinity
leaking all over
that brand new suit
An elegy for the blues
that was
Of passin' on
and pushin' through

Ooooooh…
how it hurts
in the beginning
But, after tha breakthrough
its all good

All that pressure
welling up from the belly
diaphragm diggin'
building friction
Yeah…
now it's churnin'
sweet like butta
Brotha, in tha zone
Hear what I'm sayin'?
This cat blowin'
bebop phraseology
a lyrical litany
of melodious invention
action ing verbs
like Dizzy cookin'
copious
continuous
noteworthy cool
This right hear
is tha sound of Jazz

Monked

If Dr. Seuss was
really hip
he may
have imagined
his cat in the hat
like this jazz cat
in pork pie lid
and scraggly beard
Monk ing around
blues tinged
Misterioso
tracing
Brilliant corners
across imaginary floorboards
Dig this ubiquitous
dissonant cool
a vocalese flow
The felonious one
chasin' the straight out
jagged rhythms turned
Bemsha Swing
moments
prompting
copacetic soles

To slide epistrophonic
into 3/4 groove
isotoner interludes
Brotha Thelonious lost
in abstract lull
asymmetric realms of
atonal key strikes
Rhythm-a-ring
the thing
into overdrive

Senor Monk just
gettin' started
high above the clouds
skippin' over
Green chimneys
swingin' tunes
we've yet to hear

Homage

It's the catch
the phrasing
carving out places
chasing lines inside phrases
bogarting bars
cramming notes
into overcrowded spaces
blistering improvisation
spilling over measures
An incendiary serenade
fervent
euphorium
dig his embouchureal
transcendent riffs
florid
and furious
postulating pauses
amid exaggerated drags
cuffing half smoked squares

cats with horns
cutting through chatter
well versed in
storied lore of Jazz

burning up changes
exploring connections
to legendary lineages
chasing the root
of trumpet players
Louie, Miles, Freddie
and Woody
the tunes they played
the sounds they made
How they blew
What they knew
New Orleans
to Be Bop
Be Bop to Cool
Hard Bop
Modal
the Avant-garde
Everything is cool
as long as it swings

Trane ing in

Impressions of Trane
mercurial madness
sheets of sound
saxophone excellence
cabaret cards
top notched geniuses
hustled into inconspicuous
back doors
front entrances
and lunch counters closed
even though
these were the headliners
Access denied
to the real groove masters
who kept the curious entertained
and fantasies attainable
responsible
for settin' shoes to tappin'
and steady dollars
to droppin'
In between sets
heads and horns bowed
forced to retreat into the background
eat in greasy
hidden

Jim Crow kitchens
and smile
while creating elaborate illusions
for lily white patrons
asserting their privilege
anxious for a taste of that
uptown flava
gettin' fat off all that

Soul food and
so called jungle music
they've heard about from friends
brave enough to climb
synthetic vines
and swing into the ghetto
rubbin' elbows with themselves
cause the only native folk
are serving drinks
or on the bandstand
the rest exiled
watching others
absorb their culture
repackage the best parts
ship it to the masses
Once the lights go out
social experiment ceases
test subjects are led back
to their cages

while observers
quickly exchange lab coats
for more appropriate attire
chasin' outgoing trains
and nervous taxi drivers
back to comfortable confines
of their Blue Note records

Bud Powell

8 bar intro
An elude
in C major
A nod to Bartok
and it's off to the races
Chick goin' in
on Tempus Fugit
I hear the ghost
of Bud Powell
fastidious precision
Corea like
a morning sprite
quick keystrokes
coaxing the most
melodious tones
tight
taut
tense uptempo
push n' pull
gradual release
fingers floating
flying
deft
darting melodic
black n'whites
a blur
furious blending

bending notes
to will
Percussionist rhythm
settin' the edge

Drum sticks crackin'
cymbals crashin'
ride, baby ride
bass drum boomin'
swingin' the cadence
that bounce
the ebullience
Bassist walkin'
a hole in my head
reminiscent of
Paul Chambers
when he played with Miles
the first great quintet
or maybe like Mingus
at Massey Hall
contagious
infectious
heads noddin'
feet tappin'
in unison
the audience
playin' catch up

pay attention
or you're gonna
get left
I believe that was the blues
that just walked in

Legendary

Nancy, with that laughing face
crooning Round Midnight
in sultry
smoky blue
or belting out
I Want to Be Happy
such marvelous phrasing
enunciating
flawlessly
pitched perfection
Them There Eyes
echoing eras of elegance
I Still Get A Kick
out of her unique
way of voicing
her countenance
exquisitely contorted
extracting
extraordinary
mellifluous tones
My One and Only Love
the perfect expression
of sound
I imagine Nancy
somewhere in the clouds

Rhythm-a-ning sublime
still singin' songs
But Not For Me
She'll be 500 Miles High
headlining at some celestial
Jazz cafe
performing
standing room only
for the heavenlies

Lazy Afternoon

Laid out
elongated on lounger
listless limbs
languishing lethargic
subconsciously submerged
remnants of the day left
a million miles behind
shades pulled
lights dimmed
I, counting notes
instead of sheep
Henderson's Tenor
burnin' the midnight oil
In 4/4 time
Each exhalation of syncopation
informing rhythm of R.E.M.
the copacetic snapping
of restless somnambulistic fingers
sleepwalking
rapid repetitive twitching
Myokymial swing
Inside irregular slumber
B flat scales
angular motion
jazzin' me along

to Langston's Jazzonia
I press repeat
fall fast asleep
and dream again

Dig

Gettin' in the groove
diggin' the rhythm
quartet ensemble
on early AM gallivant
These cats goin' in
sundown
to sun up
Jazz
the turn up
a blowin' session burnout
pure and simple
where the casualties of war
are the musicians
who thought they could
but, couldn't
Ain't no second chances here
Cats cuttin' creases into rivals
crazy enough to match wits
or trade notes
It's standing room only
the hottest ticket in town
No rules
just music
show me them bars
Each session

a five minute showdown
full sprint
full tilt
the race to the finish line
a short one
but, it'll damn sure
wake you up
got cats somersaulting
over tabletops

Bass, Drum, and Piano hits
Tenor riff(ed) up
roughing up
the competition
with ridiculous runs
in concordant
reckless abandon
cats cookin'
chasin' impeccable cool
that incessant swing
tha real stanky wanky
the hip hanky panky
It's rise n fly
win, you in
lose, hit the door
Who's got next.

Litter Box Blues

Foregoing
the traditional
for something wild
outside the box
an abstract blues
scratched 12 bars in
This vocalese scat cat
goin ham
hip
cat-nipped
three sheets to the wind
searching for a Dolores
of his own
to dream about
a feline
femme fatale
claws bared
whiskers whipped
meowing discordant melodiousness
in every measure
bar after bar
no let up
no pauses

Kitty cornering keys

with dissonant ease
rhythm-a-ning
the swing
Thelonious like
licking paws
pitch purrfect purring
in between phrases
chasing scales
instead of tails
no playin' it straight
The groove incendiary
burnin
uptempo
One down
8 lives to go

Revival

Black, brown
and beautiful
an evocative tribute
Enlightened
nu negroes
doin' it big
melanin poppin'
souls emboldened
busy
bustlin'
struttin' uptown
welcome to New York
a renaissance is brewin'
Brownstones and bodegas
echoes of Harlem
the "above it all's"
hustlin' down to Sugar Hill
and Striver's Row
Visions of Langston on Lenox
and 125th
The motion of music
words and rhythm
shut up in bones
shoutin' fiyaaah
at top of soulful lungs

Jessie B Semple's
not a nickel between them
chattin' up the ladies
then, down to Duke's place
Big band roots
reveling in swingdom
Black n Tan fantasies
and Creole love songs
spillin' into anxious ears
Ghosts of Lindy hoppers
leapin' over rhythms
all knees and elbows
on overcrowded dance floors
Now, just empty ballrooms
blues in the bag
from bygone eras

Andrew Hill Interlude

It's Noon Tide
when Passing Ships
Cascade
in and out
of step
casting Sideways
aspersions at
Brown eyed Queens
sitting high
upon the shore
Carpet Bags packed
with promises
leaving plantation nightmares
behind
Yesterday's
hidden among
scented magnolias
pride stretched across
weary shoulders
hoping this
will be the day
dreams come true

Left Hand Lacey

Late again
No left
go right
wrong again
One step behind
but gaining ground
In the eye of a hurricane
riding the storm
cookin' with every euphonious
turning over
of note
gobbling up changes
swingin' tunes
off its hinges
broad smile
electricity
in his fingers
straddling line
between barrelhouse
and stride
an ol skool
Contemporary vibe

left riffin runs
right compin' behind
coloring the groove
stretchin' the pace

jumpin' the ivories
the history of jazz piano
on tips of calloused fingers
commandeering keystrokes
left hand dancin'
cigarette danglin'
One eye on the chart
The other front row
stealin' winks at
the club owners wife
hoping for some company
after the show..

Hooked

Art and addiction
the dark seduction
Off the planet
cerebral's gettin' fried
chasin' spotlight highs
and hard bop lines
laced heroin
habitual
Imagination
and keys cookin'
gotta a jones
in the bones
for sumthin' beyond
the hallucinatory
In hot pursuit of
that elusive swing
slingin' improvised figments
till the next fix kicks
Straight up n' down
on pawn shop promenade
A game of
musical chairs
instruments on parade
gotta connect with them ends
shootin' up n' gettin' high
pushin' needles
into veins

cramped with ideas
craving inspiration
imaginary notes
and voices
plucked from
psychedelic hazes
in a syncopated daze

searching for innovative
ways of playin'
new ways of hearing
far out cadences
and phrases
tappin' into a new creativity
cause you can't get there
on your own
Need three more tracks
to finish this album
Psst...
Hey my brotha
I got sumthin' for ya

Miles to Go

Advancing the notion
pain begets promise
Consider...
the immodest cool
of a black prince exiled
in manic pursuit
of a level playing field
blowin' internalized
modal angst
notes dispersed
in acerbic bursts
solitary rebellious growls
eviscerating modern
social convention
Miles ahead
refusing to bow
not disguised
in guise of
compromise

Miles blew his truth loud
out in the open
horn his voice
no excuses
At 19 learning
lessons of jazzhood
next to Bird

Max
Diz
and Bud
The etiquette of the day
never look them
straight in the eye
and never forget
your cabaret card
Otherwise...
get your head busted in
fresh blood trickles
First fruits
of revolution

Elegy for a Pharoah

The creator had
a master plan
imbuing this majestic
man of Jazz
A Saxophonist supreme
summoning ancestors
and us
Tenor his bullhorn
a clarion call
urgent rushing of notes
invoking invocations
innovative interventions
cutting edge
intercessory prayer
blowin' distinctive
sheets of sound
akin to Trane
then chasing the same
alongside Albert Ayler
into consecrated
Jazz sainthood

Father and Holy Ghost
Pharoah, the Son
A disciple of the Wise One
spreading spiritual fire
a call to worship

incendiary benediction
Avant-garde sermons
Karma laden notions
Laced with Jewels of thought
An Ascension into
celestial mediations
and a beautiful beyond

I Remember

In the small hours
Jazz heads commiserating
over drinks
Mister Hubbard liftin' spirits
elucidating tones
straight up n' down
and juxtaposed
fingertips flippin' fluid over valves
phrases flowin' furiously
spewing incendiary streams
of expired air
churnin'
burnin'
notes outnumbered
wholes, halves, and quarters
blown out of order
floating
fluttering over bass riffs
and floorboards
settin' tha pace
The night Freddie Hubbard blew
the roof off the place

Jazz Sketch

A cypher
sittin' atop syntax
Improvising ad libs
in between phrases
Transforming riffs
into stanzas
an ode to an art form
expressions of erudition
Ars Poetica
Scion of the slick literali
Loquacious
linguistic
Nouveau soul lingua franca
My nom de plume
Pen game insane
Riffin like a Jazz musician
open ended
free improvisation
spontaneous invention
these lines impromptu
euphonious
just listen to the cadence
of my iambic pentameter
droppin' vocabulary
like instrumental solos

too much dialogue
to fit in a measure
so, I improvise words
instead of notation
tappin' into swing vernacular
Jazz my muse
cogent
cool
I cut my poetic teeth
on Harlem Renaissance poets

combining Langston's meter
with Coltrane's modal configurations
rhyme and rhythm
set to a groove
the barz
the vibe
the flow
and the music

Me n' Mingus

Attempting to mimic
the mind of Mingus
engage his genius
tap into his hiptitude
droppin the bottom
that bounce
that rhythm
low end swingin'
bass strings hammered
plucked and strummed
searching for the perfect note
beautifully calloused fingers
crossing over fretless bridges
creeping into corridors
Ambulation spectacular
accelerating double time
Mr. Mingus gallivanting
walkin' the dawg
turning tonics
bangin' Big band explorations
on the cool side of blue
slidin' soul infected fingers
up n'down
Worn weathered wood
Mingus Ah Um

raising bones of elders

And me…

trying to get hit in my soul

Abstrakt

The very thought
of harmonic thinking
abstract notions
linking contrapuntal complexities
dissonant cool
purposely off kilter
An ensemble assembled
in perfect disarray
driving subversive
syncopated rhythms
Dig this ugly beautiful
Aaaaah…
Tense
tight
taut
A conscious cacophony
the art of noise
on mellifluous display
densely packed notes
sublimely grotesque
Sharps cutting into flats
Phrases lambasting unabated
loudly lamenting
freedom fast forwarded
rage rumbling over

root(ed) chord play
fastidious
and free
Simon says freeze
Riffs outward bound
floating through space
Tight rope ing tonality
sans the net
rushing ambulatory
swingin' between bars
dissonant lines
playin' hide n seek
cramming notes into measures
immersed in asymmetrical irregular grooves
caught up in a pulchritudinous
euphoric epiphany

Jesse B. Semple (Alternate Take)

Like a Langston Hughes
uptempo blues
long
lanky
a congenial facsimile
connoisseur
of the common
the every man's shadow
the likeness uncanny
plain folk livin'
chasin' that uptown swing
Straight, without the chaser
A lackadaisical
languid cat
slight bounce
In his step
ambulating up n down
Lenox & 125th
You can always catch him languishing
in the excitement
of the day
lingering
loose
suit jacket under arm
in leisurely vertical repose

loafer's run over
second hand rags
danglin' precariously
in dire need
of a tailor
leaking
loquaciousness
always full of chatter
never one
to run out of banter
panhandlin' for the handouts
In Harlem's low rent district
wishing he
was somebody else

After Hours

A convergence
of notes
groove uptempo
easy…
Ain't it funky
bass man walkin'
roaming down to root
piano man seducing the ivories
racing moon's farewell
into small hours
percussionist sticks
guiding the rhythm
Timepiece on the wall
signaling last rounds
and end of encores
the set ended
hours ago
now they play
solely for themselves

no special requests
no extended versions
just turnin' over of chairs
closin' of exits
and silhouettes of

incandescent strangers
stranglers
following trails
of exaggerated drags
to nowhere
half smoked squares
their pilot lights
dimmed to embers
but, enough to slip
or stumble
their way out
lonely front entrances
into silence

ABOUT THIS BOOK

In this, his first full collection of poetry, author Preston K. Touchstone drew inspiration from the work of artists who emerged during the Harlem Renaissance, the Beat Generation, and the Black Arts Movement.

His use of elements like jazz rhythms and vernacular language, follow the unique form of iconic writers like Langston Hughes, Ted Joans, Jayne Cortez, Yusuf Komunyakaa and Amiri Baraka. Writers whose voices and contributions brilliantly depicted the joys, struggles, art, music and complexities of the African-American experience and continue to speak to it today.

Notes from the Underground continues this tradition of cultural celebration through the arts.

ABOUT THE AUTHOR

Preston's poetry has been published in the international journal, *Network 2000: In the Spirit of the Harlem Renaissance* and the anthology, *Togther As One Voice...We Speak.*

Preston currently resides in his hometown city of Milwaukee, Wisconsin. You can find more of this poets work on Instagram @fred_e_freeloader

www.ingramcontent.com/pod-product-compliance
Lightning Source LLC
Chambersburg PA
CBHW070939160426
43193CB00011B/1740